For my mother and father

William Heinemann Limited
10 Upper Grosvenor Street, London W 1X 9PA
LONDON MELBOURNE TORONTO JOHANNESBURG AUCKLAND

First published 1984
Concept, design and illustration © Jan Pieńkowski 1984
434 495649 X

Christmas

The King James Version
with pictures
by

Jan Pieńkowski

HEINEMANN : LONDON

IN THE DAYS of Herod the King,
the angel Gabriel was sent from God
unto a city named Nazareth, to a virgin
espoused to a man whose name was Joseph;

and the virgin's name was Mary.

AND THE ANGEL said,
Thou shalt bring forth a son,
and shalt call his name Jesus. He shall be called
the Son of the Highest: and of his kingdom
there shall be no end.

And Mary said, Behold the handmaid of the
Lord. And the angel departed from her.

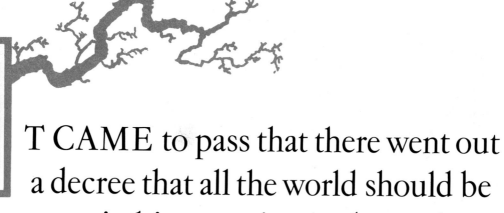

IT CAME to pass that there went out a decree that all the world should be taxed, every one in his own city. And Joseph went up from Nazareth to the city called Bethlehem, to be taxed with Mary his wife, being great with child.

AND SHE brought forth
her firstborn son, and wrapped him
in swaddling clothes, and laid him in a manger;
because there was no room for them
in the inn.

There were in the same country shepherds
keeping watch over their flock by night.
And the angel of the Lord came upon them,
and they were sore afraid.

And the angel said unto them, Fear not:
I bring you good tidings of great joy.
For unto you is born a Saviour, which is Christ
the Lord. And this shall be a sign unto you;
ye shall find the babe wrapped in swaddling clothes,
lying in a manger.

SUDDENLY there was a multitude
of the heavenly host saying, Glory
to God in the highest, and on earth peace,
good will toward men.

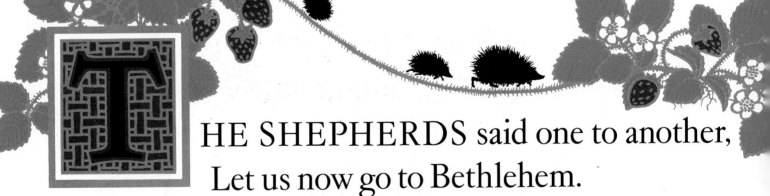

THE SHEPHERDS said one to another,
Let us now go to Bethlehem.
And they found Mary, and Joseph, and the babe
lying in a manger.

And all they that heard it wondered at those
things which were told them by the shepherds.
But Mary kept all these things, and pondered them
in her heart.

And the shepherds returned, praising God.

BEHOLD, there came wise men from the east, saying, Where is he that is born King of the Jews? For we have seen his star in the east, and are come to worship him.

When Herod the King heard these things, he was troubled. And he sent them to Bethlehem, and said, Go and search diligently for the child; and when ye have found him, bring me word again, that I may come and worship him also.

WHEN THEY had heard the King, they departed; and lo, the star went before them, till it stood over where the young child was.

And they saw the young child with Mary
his mother, and fell down and worshipped him;
and when they had opened their treasures,
they presented unto him gifts:
gold, and frankincense, and myrrh.

Being warned in a dream that they should
not return to Herod, they departed into their
own country another way.

AND THE ANGEL appeared
to Joseph in a dream, saying, Arise,
and take the child and his mother, and flee
into Egypt, for Herod will seek the child
to destroy him.

When he arose, he took the child and his mother by night, and departed into Egypt.

THEN HEROD was exceeding wroth,
and sent forth and slew
all the children that were in Bethlehem,
from two years old and under.
Then was there lamentation and weeping
and great mourning.

BUT WHEN Herod was dead, an angel
appeared in a dream to Joseph
in Egypt, saying, Take the child and his mother,
and go into the land of Israel: for they are dead
which sought the young child's life.

And he took the child and his mother, and came
into the land of Israel, and dwelt in Nazareth.

ND THE CHILD grew, and waxed strong in spirit, filled with wisdom: and the grace of God was upon him.

Editor, Judith Elliott
The illustrator would like to thank the following for their help:
Rowena Hart, Robert Roper, Hilary Saunders and Jane Walmsley

Printed in Singapore by the Tien Wah Press